SPACE EXPLORERS
ROVERS

by Jenny Fretland VanVoorst

Ideas for Parents and Teachers

Pogo Books let children practice reading informational text while introducing them to nonfiction features such as headings, labels, sidebars, maps, and diagrams, as well as a table of contents, glossary, and index.

Carefully leveled text with a strong photo match offers early fluent readers the support they need to succeed.

Before Reading

- "Walk" through the book and point out the various nonfiction features. Ask the student what purpose each feature serves.
- Look at the glossary together. Read and discuss the words.

Read the Book

- Have the child read the book independently.
- Invite him or her to list questions that arise from reading.

After Reading

- Discuss the child's questions. Talk about how he or she might find answers to those questions.
- Prompt the child to think more. Ask: Did you know that two Mars rovers, Spirit and Opportunity, were named by an elementary schooler? What would you name a space rover?

Pogo Books are published by Jump!
5357 Penn Avenue South
Minneapolis, MN 55419
www.jumplibrary.com

Copyright © 2017 Jump!
International copyright reserved in all countries.
No part of this book may be reproduced in any form without written permission from the publisher.

Library of Congress Cataloging-in-Publication Data

Names: Fretland VanVoorst, Jenny, 1972- author.
Title: Rovers / by Jenny Fretland VanVoorst.
Description: Minneapolis, MN: Jump!, Inc. [2016]
Series: Space explorers | Audience: Ages 7-10.
Includes bibliographical references and index.
Identifiers: LCCN 2016021008 (print)
LCCN 2016021946 (ebook)
ISBN 9781620314159 (hardcover: alk. paper)
ISBN 9781624964626 (ebook)
Subjects: LCSH: Roving vehicles (Astronautics)—Juvenile literature. | Space Robotics—Juvenile literature.
Mars (Planet)—Exploration—Juvenile literature.
Classification: LCC TL475 .F74 2016 (print)
LCC TL475 (ebook) | DDC 629.43/5—dc23
LC record available at https://lccn.loc.gov/2016021008

Editor: Kirsten Chang
Book Designer: Molly Ballanger
Photo Researcher: Kirsten Chang

Photo Credits: Age Fotostock, cover; Alamy, 1, 6-7, 8-9, 10, 11, 16-17; Edwin Verin/Shutterstock.com, 4; Getty, 3, 14-15; NASA, 18; Science Source, 20-21, 23; Shutterstock, 5, 16-17; Superstock, 12-13, 19.

Printed in the United States of America at Corporate Graphics in North Mankato, Minnesota.

TABLE OF CONTENTS

CHAPTER 1

GETTING THERE

How do we know what rocks are on Mars? How can we see its mountains and valleys? Rovers!

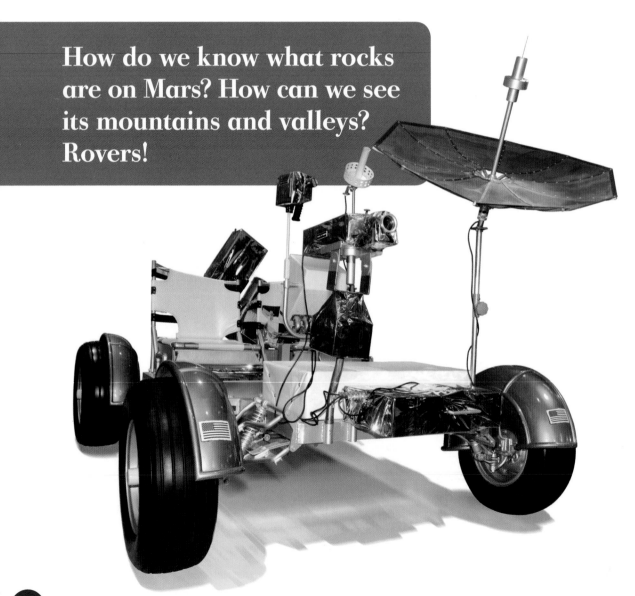

A rover is a special kind of spacecraft. It is built to move across the surface of an alien planet.

Some carry members of a human crew. One carried **astronauts** across the moon's surface. Others have been **autonomous** robots.

Rovers work on other planets. But they are built here on Earth. How does a rover that starts in a lab on Earth get to a valley on Mars? It travels in the nose of a **rocket**.

lander

It sits inside a **lander**. This is a special shell that houses the rover. When the lander drops, rockets fire. They slow it down.

Air bags inflate. They surround the lander. When it hits the ground, the rover inside is safe.

CHAPTER 2

· ·

ROVERS AT WORK

Once on a planet's surface, the rover's job begins. Scientists want to learn whether other planets can support life.

Rovers gather **data** to help find the answer. They have tools that let them drill into the ground.

They can gather rocks.
They can take pictures.
They can even even
analyze what they
find on-site.

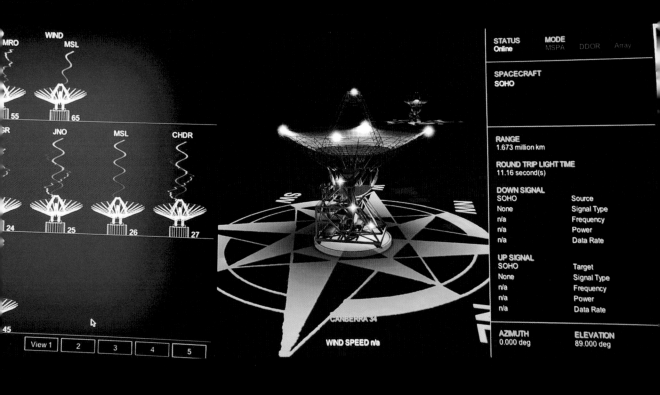

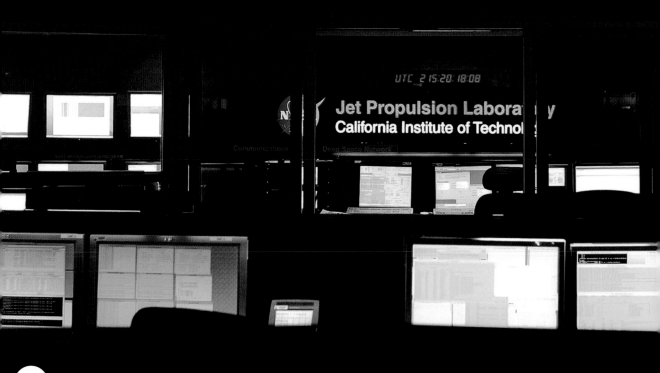

ANT	START
14	215/19:4
GR 24	215/13:35
25	215/14:20
26	215/19:40
DR 27	215/21:00
HO 34	215/20:55
WN 43	215/18:10
R2 45	215/17:00
1O 54	215/15:10
RO 55	215/13:00
SL 63	215/11:35
SL 65	215/11:40

215/20:17

Other tools help connect them with Earth. People on Earth can have the rover gather certain samples. They can have it do an experiment. They can change the rover's path.

But the rover is very far away. It takes a long time for a message to be received. This means there's a lot that it has to do on its own.

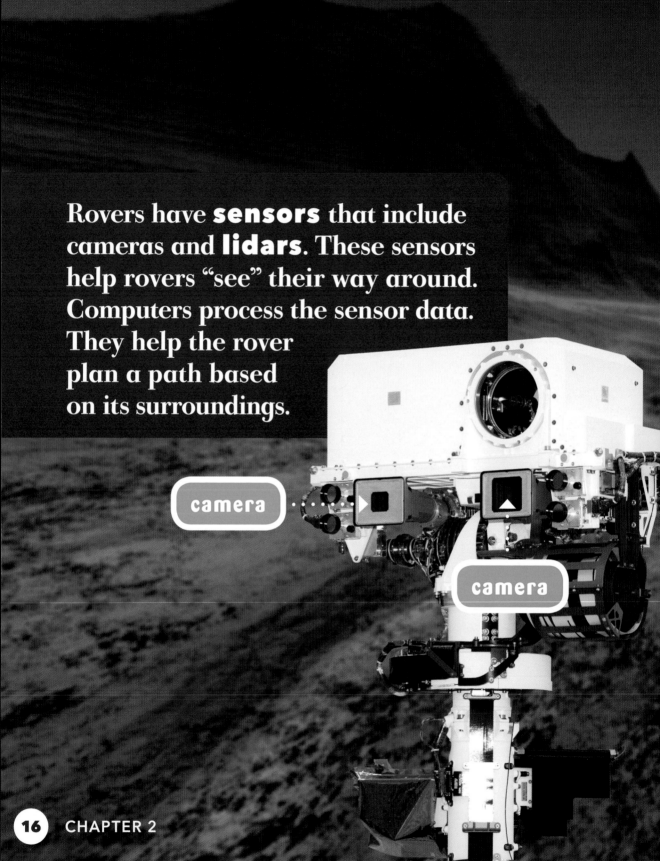

Rovers have **sensors** that include cameras and **lidars**. These sensors help rovers "see" their way around. Computers process the sensor data. They help the rover plan a path based on its surroundings.

camera

camera

Rovers are covered in sensors and tools.

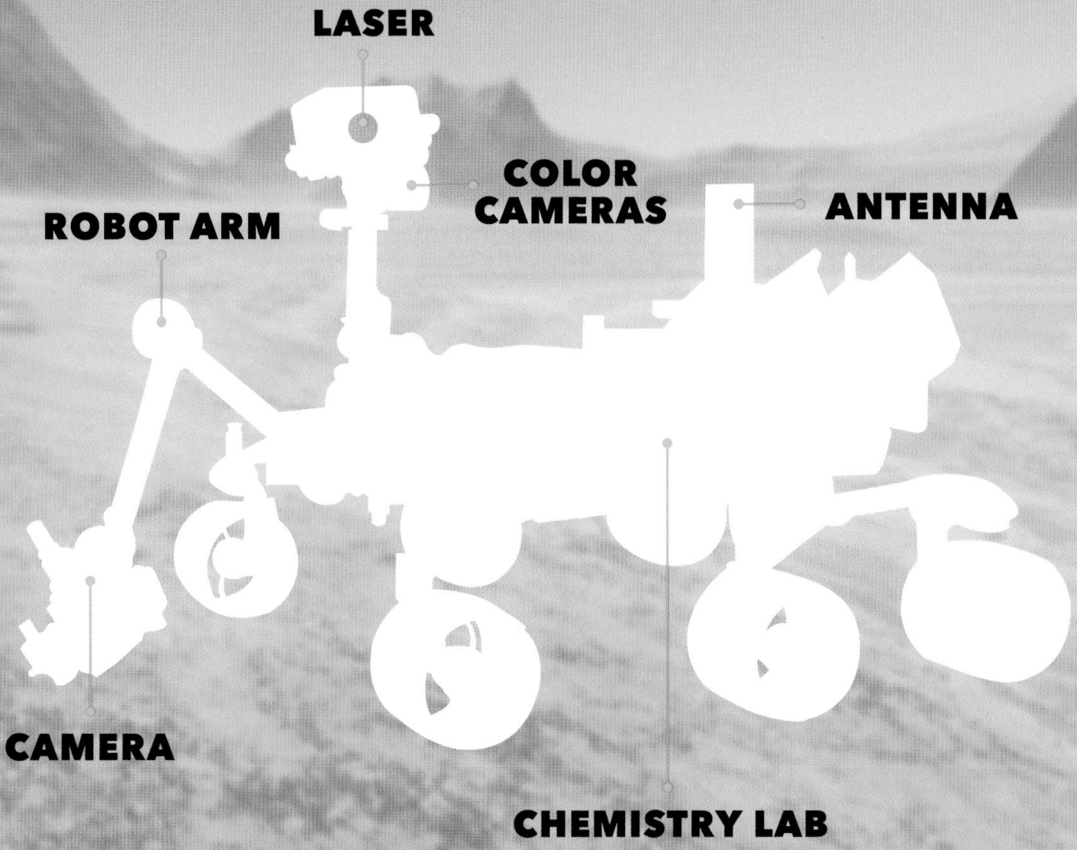

LASER

COLOR CAMERAS

ANTENNA

ROBOT ARM

CAMERA

CHEMISTRY LAB

CHAPTER 3

MEET THE
ROVERS

Today rovers are at work on the surface of Mars. Opportunity went there in 2004 to look for signs of life. It is still working today.

Opportunity

In March 2015 it had traveled 26.2 miles (42 kilometers). That's farther than any other rover. It's also the length of a marathon! Its finish time was 11 years and 2 months.

Curiosity

A rover named Curiosity is on Mars as well. It is studying the planet's **climate**. It studies its rocks. It takes samples. It does experiments.

Because of rovers, we know things about Mars we otherwise never could.

DID YOU KNOW?

China put a rover on the moon in 2013. It is called Chang'e 3. It is still there, collecting data.

ACTIVITIES & TOOLS

PROGRAM A ROVER

Because rovers operate at such a great distance from people, they need very clear programs to follow in order to do their work. Pretend your friend is a rover, and write a program for him or her to complete. You won't discover life on Mars, but you'll end up with a tasty sandwich!

What You Need:
- peanut butter
- two slices of bread
- jam or jelly (optional)
- butter knife
- pencil and paper

1 **Write down the steps needed to make a peanut butter sandwich.**

2 **Then ask a friend to follow the steps exactly, without taking anything for granted or making any assumptions.**

3 **For example, it is not enough to ask your friend to reach for the peanut butter. How far should she extend her arm? Should she angle it up or down? How much? When should she grasp the jar? When should she let go?**

4 **How far did your friend get before there was a problem? Record the error and replan. Then rewrite the instructions, and try again.**

air bags: Protective devices consisting of a bag designed to inflate automatically in order to cushion a rover against impact.

analyze: To study a thing in order to discover its parts and the relationships among them.

astronauts: People who have been trained to fly aboard a spacecraft and work in space.

autonomous: Able to make certain decisions without human input.

climate: Typical weather conditions.

data: Facts about something that can be used in calculating, reasoning, or planning.

lander: A protective shell that surrounds a rover and controls and cushions its descent.

lidars: Devices that use laser beams to detect and locate objects.

rocket: A space vehicle that is driven through the air by the gases produced by a burning substance.

sensors: Onboard equipment that serves as a robot's eyes, ears, and other sense organs so that the robot can create a picture of the environment in which it operates.

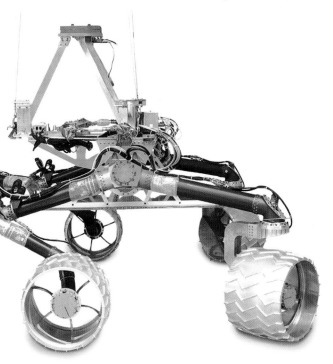

INDEX

TO LEARN MORE

Learning more is as easy as 1, 2, 3.

1) Go to www.factsurfer.com

2) Enter "rovers" into the search box.

3) Click the "Surf" button to see a list of websites.

With factsurfer, finding more information is just a click away.